Root English

Book 2

Magic Coin

Magic Finger

Magic Tree House

Toem Books

John Stephen Knodell

ISBN – 978-4-908152-13-9

Toem Books
Tel. 011-839-3771
Email. info@to-em.com
札幌市中央区北２条西２６丁目２番１８号　２６ＷＥＳＴビル　４F-A

www.to-em.com

Dedicated to

Yurika, Yura, Haruki and Reo

How to Use the Book

The Blossom English series is a content-based textbook that uses authentic readings with grammar, writing, and speaking exercises. While the textbook is rich with grammar exercises, exercises can be used to A) create conversations from the grammar exercises B) test students on the problematic grammar points throughout the book, and C) connect the reading book with sections of the textbook, for example, the making perfect sentences and grammar focus sections.

For classes studying English approximately 3-4 hours a week, try to finish one reading section, one grammar focus/preposition/article exercise, and one writing assignment. Each week, test students on one of the grammar exercises, have a review test of the vocabulary, and always use the textbook as an opportunity to speak with students. In order to prepare for writing essays, debate the topic before giving the assignment for homework.

About the Author

John Stephen Knodell has an M.Ed. in TESOL, and has been an English language teacher for over 20 years. He has taught students from 2 years old to students over 80, from private classes to classes of over 100 students. He currently teaches at a university in Japan.

TABLE OF CONTENTS

Reading
Section

Chanmee

VOCABULARY TO LEARN

alone, except, bothering, tough, scary, didn't care, searching for, hide, forest,

climbing, crawled, swing, vine

QUESTIONS

1. Where did Chanmee live?

2. Who wasn't nice to her?

3. What kind of book was she reading?

4. How did Chanmee leave her tree (i.e. by car, on foot...)?

5. What did Chanmee take with her?

King Kong

VOCABULARY TO LEARN

cave, map, staring, nodded, searched, grabbed, curly hair, bright, suddenly, sadness

QUESTIONS

1. What was Kong holding?

2. Was the cave noisy?

3. Why did Kong get angry?

4. What is wrong with Shong?

5. Why did Kong want to get the coin?

Julia

VOCABULARY TO LEARN

changed into, special power, squirrel, upset, decided, eagle, chirped, shrieked, just in

case, thirsty

QUESTIONS

1. What was Julia's special power?

2. How did the small bird feel?

3. What kind of bird did Julia change into?

4. What was Julia and the bird's plan?

5. Why did Julia take the kulu juice?

Eric

VOCABULARY TO LEARN

hungry, climbed, both, tasty, bushes, whispered, fishing rod, cast, hook, lifted,

completely quiet, nervously, branch, he missed

QUESTIONS

1. How often was Eric hungry?

2. Where was Eric?

3. How many monkeys were following Chanmee?

4. How did Chanmee get in the tree?

5. Did Eric miss the monkey that took Chanmee's bag?

6. Why was Eric crying?

Stinky Mountain

VOCABULARY TO LEARN

make trouble, in fact, afraid of, got lost, followed, however, squirted, a cricket,

blindly, shook, terrible, rule the world, ant, tail, thirsty

QUESTIONS

1. What animal did Julia never change into?

2. Why was Julia afraid of kiwis?

3. Why didn't Julia see her family again?

4. A long time ago, what kind of boy was Kong?

5. When did Julia and Kong stop playing together?

6. How did Julia slow down the monkey with the pink bag?

7. What did the monkey look like?

8. What hit the monkey on the head?

9. Was Stev a kind teacher?

10. How did Stev control Kong?

Meeting

VOCABULARY TO LEARN

steal, surprised, change into, shocked, dropped, fluffy clouds, near, angrily, huge,

claws

QUESTIONS

1. Where did Julia go to find Chanmee and Eric?

2. What was Eric doing when he met Julia?

3. Why was Julia surprised about Chanmee?

4. What does Julia want to do for Chanmee?

5. What kind of bird did Julia change into?

Teacher Stev

VOCABULARY TO LEARN

yelled, cave, incredibly, grim, fridge, porridge, whispered, stared, empty eyes

QUESTIONS

1. What was Kong doing when the monkey ran into the cave?

2. What did Stev never do?

3. Why did Stev tell Kong to wait?

4. Did Stev use magic on Kong?

5. How did Shong feel when Stev used magic on her brother?

The Escape

VOCABULARY TO LEARN

whispered, mad, stomach, a secret hole, snake, frozen, ran like a cheetah, on his way,

shiny, a whistle, hairy, bend down, spears, axe, safety

QUESTIONS

1. Why was Eric sad?

2. What did Julia change into?

3. Did they go up or down the secret hole?

4. Why did Chanmee tell Eric about the sandwich?

5. How fast did Eric run to get the sandwich?

6. How did Kong feel when he woke up?

7. Why did Eric start to cry?

8. What did Kong do with his whistle?

9. How big was Yurgly's head?

10. At the end, why did Kong stop talking?

Summary

Going Home

VOCABULARY TO LEARN

landed, complained, shine, licking his lips, shouted, looking for, meaner, bald guy,

waved

QUESTIONS

1. How did Chanmee make the sandwich?

2. Was Eric happy about the sandwich?

3. Where did Chanmee have to go?

4. Was Chanmee worried about Kong, Stev, and the giant? If no, why not?

5. Why was Chanmee happy?

Stinky Mountain Again

VOCABULARY TO LEARN

let, scary, mean, a mess, your fault, cure you, forever, a plan

QUESTIONS

1. Why was Stev so angry?

2. How did Shong feel about Stev yelling at her brother?

3. What did Shong tell Stev to eat?

4. If Kong gets the coin, what will he do with it?

5. What did you think about this story?

Chapter 1

P.7

VOCABULARY TO LEARN

farm, owned, as best I can, hunting, woods, shoot, can't stand, talk them out of it, deer,

made me cross

QUESTIONS

1. Where does the girl live?

2. What can't she stand?

3. How much older is William compared to the girl?

4. Which animal did the Greggs kill?

5. What did the girl put on the Gregg family?

Chapter 2

VOCABULARY TO LEARN

stupid, the corner, guess what?, whiskers, screaming, a tail, huge, bushy

QUESTIONS

1. Which word did Mrs. Winter ask the girl to spell?

2. What kind of teacher was Mrs. Winter?

3. Were Mrs. Winter's whiskers smaller than a cat's?

4. What kind of tail did Mrs. Winter have?

5. What do you think Mrs. Winter looks like now?

Chapter 3

VOCABULARY TO LEARN

when I see red, tingle, a sort of, flash, electric, the whole, afternoon, headed towards,

lake, joy

QUESTIONS

1. How long has the girl had the magic finger?

2. How does she feel when the magic finger comes to her?

3. Does the magic finger only go to people who make her angry?

4. Can she stop the magic finger?

5. How many ducks did the Greggs shoot?

Chapter 4

VOCABULARY TO LEARN

missed, asking for it, dark, carrying, would not leave them alone, around and around, be

off, thin, afraid

QUESTIONS

1. Did the Greggs hit the 4 ducks?

2. What surprised everybody?

3. Why did Mr. Gregg think they missed hitting the ducks?

4. Why did Mr. Gregg get angry?

5. Why did Mr. Gregg go outside at night?

Chapter 5

VOCABULARY TO LEARN

lay still, looked like, yell, wings, instead of, sobbed, witches, flapping their wings, burst in,

tiny, all at once

QUESTIONS

1. Who woke up first?

2. What body part changed on the Gregg family?

3. How tall was Mr. Gregg?

4. Why were Philip and William so happy?

5. Was Mrs. Gregg getting tired flying in the sky?

Chapter 6

VOCABULARY TO LEARN

below, enormous, beaks, quacked, foxes, a nest, must, chose, sticks, mouths, stick

together

QUESTIONS

1. How big were the ducks?

2. Why did Mrs. Gregg sob?

3. What did William want to do?

4. What was Mr. Gregg's plan?

5. What did they need to build their new home?

Chapter 7

VOCABULARY TO LEARN

leaves, feathers, hopping, at last, tin of biscuits, pecked to bits, worms, slugs, disgusting,

bites

QUESTIONS

1. How was their new home?

2. Why couldn't the Greggs go into their old home?

3. What were the ducks doing?

4. Could the Greggs eat the apples?

5. Why did the Greggs go back to their nest?

Chapter 8

VOCABULARY TO LEARN

tried to, a voice, a great wind, blow, the tree rocked, rained and rained, the side, peeped,

pointing

QUESTIONS

1. Was the girl worried about Philip and his family?

2. What funny sound did she hear?

3. Which happened first, the rain or the wind?

4. What did Mrs. Gregg never want to do again?

5. Why were the Greggs shocked?

Chapter 9

Vocabulary to Learn

allowed to, do you mean that?, as long as I live, give me your word, throw away, tiny bits,

congratulate you

Questions

1. What did Mr. and Mrs. Gregg tell the ducks not to do?

2. How many baby ducks were shot yesterday?

3. What did Mr. Gregg promise?

4. What will Mr. Gregg do with his guns?

5. Did the ducks think the Greggs' nest was bad?

Chapter 10

VOCABULARY TO LEARN

all at once, couldn't see, bright, back to normal, come back, glad, joy, wild duck, heading, a

queer sight, smashing, graves, a sack of, scattering

QUESTIONS

1. After they changed, where were the Greggs standing?

2. How do you know the Greggs were happy?

3. When the girl went to the Greggs' house, what was Mr. Gregg doing?

4. What was Mrs. Gregg putting on the graves?

5. What were the boys feeding the birds?

Chapter 11

VOCABULARY TO LEARN

feather, completely, dotty, proudly, it's a mess, up to the brim, loud, tingling, what's up?

QUESTIONS

1. What was Mr. Gregg's new name?

2. Did the girl think the Greggs were crazy?

3. What was Mr. Gregg proud of?

4. How did the Greggs' bathroom look?

5. Why did the girl run away?

6. What was the best part of the story?

Chapter 1

VOCABULARY TO LEARN

monster, pretend, watch out, race you, the woods, sun set, disappeared, groaned, ladder,

branches, sighed

QUESTIONS

1. How old is Annie?

2. What kind of things does Jack like?

3. In the story, what time is it?

4. What did Annie find?

5. Why did Jack like the tree house?

Chapter 2

VOCABULARY TO LEARN

crawl, filled with, dusty, shiny, peering, porch, tiny, glanced, castle, ancient reptile, wings,

gliding, beak, spinning

QUESTIONS

1. What kind of books were in the tree house?

2. What color is Jack and Annie's house?

3. Who owns the books?

4. Why did Annie scream?

5. At the end, what did the tree house start to do?

Chapter 3

VOCABULARY TO LEARN

exactly the same, soaring, a hill, volcano, creature, spinning, a guard, ancient

QUESTIONS

1. Was the picture in the book and outside the tree house the same?

2. Does Annie think everything is real?

3. Where was the Pteranodon standing?

4. Why does Jack think Annie is crazy?

5. When did dinosaurs live?

Chapter 4

VOCABULARY TO LEARN

gasped, crest, stroked, examine, stare, alert, cautiously, a bean, jaws, scissors, huge

QUESTIONS

1. Why did Jack go to see the dinosaur?

2. What did Annie want Jack to do?

3. Was the Pteranodon's skin hard?

4. Does Jack think the dinosaur is dumb?

5. At the end, why was Annie surprised?

Chapter 5-1

VOCABULARY TO LEARN

push, quit it, scrambled, tumbled, huge, horns, are you nuts, sighed, shoulder, kneeled,

peeked out

QUESTIONS

1. Why were Jack and Annie afraid?

2. Where was the huge dinosaur standing?

3. How many horns did the dinosaur have?

4. Did the triceratops eat meat?

5. How big was the triceratops?

Chapter 5-2

Vocabulary to Learn

nudged, ignored, teasing, gazed, grunted, a medallion, engraved

Questions

1. How does the triceratops eat?

2. What did Annie say to the triceratops?

3. What did Jack find in the grass?

4. What letter was on the medallion?

5. How many dinosaurs did Jack and Annie see so far?

Chapter 6-1

VOCABULARY TO LEARN

staring at, clutching, disappeared, a tuba, nests, froze, crawl, chew, bowed

QUESTIONS

1.   What was Annie doing when Jack talked to her?

2.   Where did Annie go?

3.   What did Annie find?

4.   Do you think the mother dinosaur was angry?

5.   How did Annie escape from (*nigeru*) the dinosaur?

Chapter 6-2

VOCABULARY TO LEARN

brain, nearby, grabbed, reached, crawling, barged, throw up, enormous

QUESTIONS

1. What is always nearby baby dinosaurs?

2. What did Annie give to the dinosaur?

3. Did some mother dinosaurs hunt (*kari*) for food?

4. Why did Jack almost throw up?

5. How big was the T-Rex?

Chapter 7

VOCABULARY TO LEARN

dashed, leaped, raised their heads, coast clear, groaned, guard, between

QUESTIONS

1. Where did Annie and Jack run to?

2. What does Jack wish for?

3. What did Jack forget?

4. Were there many Anatosauruses in the valley?

5. Why couldn't Jack go back to the tree house?

Chapter 8

Vocabulary to Learn

heart, jaws, knives, bite, stampede, flapping, shadow, gliding, overhead

Questions

1. Where were the duck-billed dinosaurs?

2. How many bites did the T-Rex need to eat a person?

3. Where was Jack hiding?

4. What was Annie's plan?

5. Was the T-Rex a heavy animal?

VOCABULARY TO LEARN

coasted down, stared at, flashing, climb on, tightly, amazing, a feather

QUESTIONS

1. What did Jack do with the Pteranodon?

2. Where was the T-Rex?

3. Did Jack almost fall off the Pteranodon?

4. Where did the Pteranodon fly?

5. How do we know Jack was happy?

6. What did Jack do with the Pteranodon?

Chapter 9-2

VOCABULARY TO LEARN

stream, slid off, wobbly, dizzy, slammed against, woods, softly, whistle

QUESTIONS

1. Where did the Pteranodon bring Jack?

2. How did Jack feel after flying?

3. Why did the tree house shake?

4. What did they need to go home?

5. What did the tree house start to do?

Chapter 10-1

VOCABULARY TO LEARN

point, peeked, no time had passed, dazed, shrugged, medallion

QUESTIONS

1. Who was calling Jack and Annie?

2. How much time passed?

3. Where was their mom standing?

4. Who did Annie think made the tree house?

5. Where was the medallion?

VOCABULARY TO LEARN

stands for, whispered, a dream, you're nuts, clasped, suddenly, for sure

QUESTIONS

1. What did Annie yell to her mom?

2. Who went down the ladder first?

3. Who are they going to tell about their adventure?

4. What will Jack and Annie do tomorrow?

5. Did you like the story? If yes, why, and if no, why not?

Grammar Focus
Section

Grammar Focus 1

All of the sentences below have mistakes. You must correct the sentences, and make them PERFECT.

1. My eyes colour is brown colour.

_____

2. In morning, I am wearing clothes everyday.

_____

3. I sometimes am tired in the Friday.

_____

4. Me like to playing the soccer.

_____

5. I was ate hamburger yesterday to my friend.

_____

6. I listen my teacher for 1 hours.

_____

7. I am having a small, black, nice shirt.

_____

8. A elephant is more bigger than mouse.

_____

9. I from the USA.

_____

10. Her is happy when weather is cloud.

_____

Grammar Focus 2

All of the sentences below have mistakes. You must correct the sentences, and make them **PERFECT**.

1. I am live in Sapporo since 2 months.

   _____

2. These day, I doesn't have no friend.

   _____

3. I will eating 2 piece of bread tomorrow's morning.

   _____

4. If it will snow tomorrow, I wear the hat.

   _____

5. How much price are your hat?

   _____

6. He talk slow.

   _____

7. Who is most tallest people in this room?

   _____

8. Where are you buy you new car?

   _____

9. When time do you called to me?

   _____

10. Why do you studying the English?

   _____

Grammar Focus 3

All of the sentences below have mistakes. You must correct the sentences, and make them PERFECT.

1. Me name are Jenny.

   _____

2. I wish I can made a wooden, big boat.

   _____

3. He is so friendly guy, so I am liking him.

   _____

4. Are you having any bug in your home?

   _____

5. I am a bad cooker, but I washing dishes very good.

   _____

6. Every time I playing the golf, I lose much balls.

   _____

7. The people must walk more slower in sidewalks.

   _____

8. Yesterday, I eat chickens on lunch.

   _____

9. At Friday, my friend sent to me a email.

   _____

10. Some of childrens are afraid dogs.

   _____

Grammar Focus 4

1. Yesterday, I go school.

_____

2. Sometime, monkey fall out tree.

_____

3. I brang a books to library in Sunday morning.

_____

4. It is tomorrow going to snowing.

_____

5. In summer, I will taking trip to USA.

_____

6. I bought a Japan, red, delicious apple today.

_____

7. I am run slow because I hurted my foot.

_____

8. We did study yesterday in me friend house.

_____

9. On Christmas, I not dancing with family.

_____

10. How long it take you doing your homeworks?

_____

Grammar Focus 5

All of the sentences below have mistakes. You must correct the sentences, and make them PERFECT.

1. Every day, I am eat a rice.

   _____

2. As soon as I came to here, I turn on light.

   _____

3. When I visited to London, I watched many nice building.

   _____

4. If I do computer, I always drink the water.

   _____

5. I have ate a lobster two time in my life.

   _____

6. The women on chair is a very pretty.

   _____

7. How often does you washing your car?

   _____

8. Can I asking you a questions?

   _____

9. Cleaning the dishes are so much funny for me.

   _____

10. I ate myself, so my house is very quietly.

   _____

Grammar Focus 6

All of the sentences below have mistakes. You must correct the sentences, and make them PERFECT.

1. I am hoping these sentence is easily for you.

2. To study English is funny, and little hardly.

3. At Christmas day, most of Canadians eat a turkey.

4. Each people in this class are much nice.

5. Mine book are blue.

6. If it snowy tomorrow, I would be wearing my blue, warm hat.

7. Almost people in Japan eat the sushi.

8. Today's are nice day.

9. I am short leg, and I can run fastly.

10. When I am feeling tired, I eat glass of coffee.

Grammar Focus 7

1. I was cut by myself when I felled down yesterday.

   _____

2. I have 2 of dictionary. One is English, but another is Spanish.

   _____

3. Nobody can't fly a airplane in my families.

   _____

4. My dog have friendly and kindly.

   _____

5. Me and my friend have not any brother.

   _____

6. I am interested at golf, but I am no good in golf.

   _____

7. I want to trip to hot country.

   _____

8. Every time we talking each other, we was laughed.

   _____

9. My mother gave to me a jean at my birthday.

   _____

10. Some of dogs like a cat.

   _____

Grammar Focus 8

All of the sentences below have mistakes. You must correct the sentences, and make them **PERFECT**.

1. Boy and girl went to walking in the street.

    _____

2. How often you watch movie every weeks.

    _____

3. How much bowl of rice do she eat every weeks?

    _____

4. How long do it takes you to brushing your hairs?

    _____

5. Which pencil in the table belong him?

    _____

6. I enjoy to eat spice foods, but not at morning.

    _____

7. Elephant is more loudly than tigers in jungle.

    _____

8. I was wash my car yesterday's afternoon.

    _____

9. A few of dogs front of my home is big.

    _____

10. It is going to rainy next morning.

    _____

Grammar Focus 9

All of the sentences below have mistakes. You must correct the sentences, and make them PERFECT.

1. Some of people likes going to shopping.

_____

2. I paint boat yesterday with friend of me.

_____

3. I am having 2 foot, so I am not so much strange.

_____

4. My TV make a lots of noises, so I want to throw out it.

_____

5. I watched yesterday a movie, and it was interested.

_____

6. Can I have piece of gums?

_____

7. Ocean has many water and fishes at it.

_____

8. None of this book are bored, so I want read it.

_____

9. First time I go to Japan, it is hot.

_____

10. In my vacation, I visited to Cuba by a airplane.

_____

Grammar Focus 10

All of the sentences below have mistakes. You must correct the sentences, and make them **PERFECT**.

1. News were excited last morning.

2. Every people don't has a tail.

3. Most of people in Korea likes to playing soccer.

4. Saki have a sister, and Saki can speaking English good.

5. I am quick walking onto my house.

6. If you are me, what will you doing?

7. On June, I will take trip in Africa.

8. Right now, I work in home in my computer.

9. One of my friend are nice.

10. I wish I can flying at sky.

Grammar Focus 11

All of the sentences below have mistakes. You must correct the sentences, and make them PERFECT.

1. On Internet, she can gets many informations.

2. Can she has a cup of water? She thirsty.

3. All people in our class is from the Japan.

4. Each boy and girl want to play piano.

5. At the morning, a birds fly on the sky.

6. She is cooked the foods very fastly.

7. At morning, Meri go to the school for study.

8. All of students hates test.

9. The United States have a lots of nice building.

10. Maths are a fun things to studying.

Grammar Focus 12

1. I sometimes am tired in the end of the weeks.

    _____

2. In future, I go to moon (I hope).

    _____

3. My sister want to buy house, but she have not money.

    _____

4. I used to playing the baseball.

    _____

5. Hana always drink Japanese, green, delicious tea.

    _____

6. The English books costs a lots of moneys.

    _____

7. I like to waking at early Sunday in the morning.

    _____

8. I went yesterday to shopping for buying some clothes.

    _____

9. This room looks like a dirty.

    _____

10. Her songing is sounded beautiful.

    _____

Grammar Focus 13

All of the sentences below have mistakes. You must correct the sentences, and make them PERFECT.

1. Next time I will go to dancing, I will bring my shoe.

_____

2. I would like visit many country in world.

_____

3. Last week, I played bowling with one of my friend.

_____

4. The man in England likes to playing football.

_____

5. My dog don't have no friend in Japanese.

_____

6. I enjoy to live in mine house.

_____

7. I wish I can flying a airplane.

_____

8. Germany is more bigger than Italy, but Italy is beautifuler.

_____

9. Please eat slow because you get sicked.

_____

10. While I ate a food, I was watched TV.

_____

Grammar Focus 14

All of the sentences below have mistakes. You must correct the sentences, and make them **PERFECT**.

1. I have a small, ugly, old, yellow car.

2. Next time I go to shopping, I buy a uniform.

3. What did you ate for dinner the last night?

4. How long more will you stayed on library.

5. At the afternoon, when time does you eat the lunch.

6. Car is more fast then a boat.

7. I want be more stronger than gorilla.

8. Friend is happy because give gift.

9. Man spoke to woman in restaurant.

10. First time I meet she, her is kind.

Grammar Focus 15

All of the sentences below have mistakes. You must correct the sentences, and make them PERFECT.

1. A lots of people enjoys to play golf.

---

2. I don't like a cat, but I am thinking they are cutie.

---

3. I need buy car, so I go shop tomorrow.

---

4. The weathers on May usually is cool.

---

5. I came to here by a bus.

---

6. I like to going to dancing, but I don't dance good.

---

7. They house is biger mine house.

---

8. I am thinking baby is cute.

---

9. I hurted my foot yesterday, so I can't running today.

---

10. Are you a busy on this Saturday?

Grammar Focus 16

All of the sentences below have mistakes. You must correct the sentences, and make them **PERFECT**.

1. As soon as I waking up, I drinking water.

    _____

2. Sam book is front of his pencil's case.

    _____

3. Every people have a mothers.

    _____

4. I want to saw long river, like Nile River.

    _____

5. A ball was hit my car, but my car okay.

    _____

6. Next week, I will going to watch movie.

    _____

7. My bicycle can ride very quick.

    _____

8. Washing dishes are not funny.

    _____

9. I can spoke the French just little.

    _____

10. Nobody wasn't late in this class this today.

    _____

Prepositions
Section

Prepositions 1

Fill in the blank
Write a proper preposition for each sentence. Sometimes, there is more than one answer.

1. I am _____ Canada.

2. I woke _____ _____ 7am today.

3. My books are _____ the table, not _____ my bag.

4. The lights are _____ our heads.

5. The map is _____ the wall.

6. We study _____ 9:30 _____ 11:30.

7. _____ TV, there is a lot _____ news _____ the weather.

8. Do you want to eat lunch _____ me?

9. I borrowed this book _____ you.

10. I came here _____ car.

11. Get _____ the train. It's leaving soon.

12. English is easy _____ me.

13. I bought my computer _____ $500. It was _____ sale.

14. Put _____ your hat, and let's go _____ the restaurant.

15. _____ Christmas, I always call my mom.

Prepositions 2

1. You are really good _____ driving.

2. Please write your name _____ the book.

3. When I walk _____ this room, I turn _____ the lights.

4. When I walk _____ a busy street, I walk slowly.

5. This table is made _____ wood.

6. The tissue is made _____ wood.

7. This building was made _____ strong men.

8. _____ winter, people eat a lot _____ soup.

9. Your tongue is _____ your mouth, and your socks are _____ your feet.

10. I have a cut _____ my finger, so I went _____ a hospital.

11. _____ night, I turn _____ the lights before I sleep.

12. I met my friend _____ a coffee shop _____ the morning.

13. That shirt looks good _____ you.

14. Can you help me _____ 2 minutes?

15. Can you give the eraser _____ me?

Prepositions 3

1. When can you come _____ my home?

2. I almost died _____ a car accident.

3. The bad guy escaped _____ the jail.

4. I had a fight _____ my friend _____ the afternoon.

5. If you stop trying, you are giving _____.

6. After talking _____ the phone, I hung _____ the phone.

7. _____ Saturday, I come here _____ foot.

8. I am jealous _____ people who are good _____ sports.

9. I can kick a ball very high _____ the sky.

10. I don't like people laughing _____ me.

11. The moon is _____ the sky, and the moon goes _____ the sun.

12. The bird is _____ that tree.

13. It's hot _____ here. Open _____ the door.

14. Put _____ the fire. Fast!!!

15. I have a question _____ you.

Prepositions 4

1. The number 5 is _____ 4 and 6.

2. He is good _____ singing, so he wants to be _____ a band.

3. He eats food _____ chopsticks, not _____ his hands.

4. She is interested _____ movies, so she wants to be _____ a movie one day.

5. You can park your car _____ the back of this building.

6. He got _____ a bus, and after 10 minutes, he got _____ the bus.

7. Don't write _____ the back of this paper.

8. Write your name _____ the top of this paper.

9. I lived _____ Monkey Island _____ 2 years.

10. Yuki looks _____ her mom, so her mom is happy _____ that.

11. I saw him standing _____ the bus stop.

12. There are many fish _____ that river.

13. I got a B _____ the test.

14. Why are you yelling _____ him?

15. I always spend money _____ cookies.

Prepositions 5

Fill in the blank
Write a proper preposition for each sentence. Sometimes, there is more than one answer.

1. _____ the bus, I sat _____ and fell asleep.

2. I have many boxes _____ tissue _____ my car.

3. I heard a good song _____ the radio.

4. I read a funny story _____ that magazine.

5. Why are you looking _____ me?

6. I lost my key, so I am looking _____ it.

7. I will buy this _____ cash.

8. _____ the afternoon, you can't see the moon _____ the sky.

9. She always buys things _____ her credit card.

10. I went downtown _____ a meeting.

11. I borrowed this book _____ a library.

12. I can't hear the music. Turn it _____.

13. I was born _____ 1991.

14. People play golf _____ summer _____ their friends.

15. The party is _____ January 25th.

Prepositions 6

Fill in the blank
Write a proper preposition for each sentence. Sometimes, there is more than one answer.

1. I always clean my room _____ myself.

2. Happy birthday. Blow _____ the candles.

3. My dog barks _____ people, so people get angry _____ me.

4. Who did you buy that _____?

5. Could you take a picture _____ me?

6. It is hard to blow _____ balloons.

7. I sometimes dance _____ my girlfriend.

8. When I came to Japan, the plane flew _____ the Pacific Ocean.

9. I don't understand your question _____ all.

10. I often read the news _____ the Internet.

11. The boy threw the ball _____ the window, and broke it.

12. While I was walking, I fell _____. Ouch!

13. The diver jumped _____ the diving board.

14. Snow is falling _____ the sky.

15. The airplane took _____ late _____ night.

Prepositions 7

1. The airplane landed _____ Narita Airport.

2. _____ January, it snows a lot, so put _____ a jacket.

3. I would like to take a trip _____ Hawaii.

4. This work is terrible. Please do it _____.

5. I was attacked _____ a dog 18 years ago.

6. The moon shines _____ the sky, especially _____ winter.

7. I think that boy is _____ love.

8. People can't live _____ food.

9. Airplanes fly _____ clouds _____ the sky.

10. I know my phone number _____ heart.

11. I always watch TV _____ the sofa.

12. People get _____ cars, and then get _____ _____ cars.

13. People get _____ buses, and then get _____ buses.

14. A Chinese restaurant is _____ the Park Hotel.

15. The party was called _____, so I was sad.

Prepositions 8

1. There is something wrong _____ my computer.

2. I usually clean _____ my home _____ Sunday morning.

3. _____ first, I didn't like cooking, but now I do.

4. I am tired _____ eating pizza.

5. My friend was _____ a movie, so now he is famous.

6. I like to eat dinner _____ home.

7. When you walk _____ a mountain, do you walk fast?

8. The ghost flew _____ the wall.

9. It is windy _____ there, so don't wear a hat.

10. I am selling my car, so it is _____ sale.

11. Water is all _____ Hokkaido because it is an island.

12. The clock is _____ the ceiling.

13. I live _____ the 3rd floor, so I walked _____ stairs everyday.

14. _____ dawn, birds wake up.

15. I hope you are having fun _____ this book.

Prepositions 9

1. _____ Christmas day, I got some presents _____ my mom.

2. I have lived _____ my home _____ a long time.

3. When I play _____ my friends, we play games _____ my computer.

4. _____ the Internet, people read things _____ the world.

5. The airplane flew _____ our heads.

6. This table is made _____ wood, and the tissue is made _____ wood.

7. The ceiling is _____ our heads, and is _____ this room.

8. When I listen _____ music, I sometimes dance _____ my boyfriend.

9. _____ the middle _____ the night, I heard a baby cry.

10. So, I woke _____ fast.

11. When I walk _____ a street, I always watch _____ _____ cars.

12. _____ July, _____ the top _____ a mountain, you can see stars.

13. _____ Halloween, children dress up _____ costumes.

14. What is the difference _____ there and their?

15. Please don't jump _____ _____ the window.

Prepositions 10

1. He arrived _____ the station _____ Sunday afternoon.

2. This pen belongs _____ me. It's my pen.

3. Can you carry these boxes _____ the stairs?

4. The boy dove _____ the diving board, and _____ the pool.

5. Can you figure _____ the answer _____ this question?

6. My back hurts. Can you pick _____ my pencil please?

7. Wait _____ me. Let's go together.

8. Somebody is knocking _____ the door. Let them _____.

9. Where is my cat? Let's look _____ my cat together.

10. Women put _____ make _____ when they go _____.

11. Can you open _____ the window? It's hot _____ here.

12. I have to pick _____ some bread _____ the store.

13. The fireman saved the boy _____ the fire.

14. Take _____ the garbage. It stinks.

15. My mother sometimes yelled _____ me when I was bad _____ my sister.

Prepositions 11

1. He walked _____ the room, took _____ his coat, and sat _____.

2. I put the letter _____ his hand. It was _____ his girlfriend.

3. I heard it _____ the radio.

4. Wait for us _____ the corner _____ the street.

5. We stopped overnight _____ Tokyo.

6. I have been working on this _____ an hour.

7. His health is getting better day _____ day.

8. I see him _____ time _____ time (sometimes).

9. The ball rolled _____ the table and _____ the floor.

10. He walked quickly _____ the door. He was _____ a hurry.

11. There is a hospital _____ _____ _____ my house.

12. The train will leave _____ five minutes.

13. I always bring my phone _____ me.

14. He will be here _____ 4 o'clock.

15. Once _____ a while I walk _____ work _____ foot.

Prepositions 12

1. Are they talking _____ the phone?

2. What are you thinking _____?

3. He looks _____ a nice guy.

4. Please speak _____. I can't hear you.

5. What kind of car are you looking _____?

6. This looks _____ a good book.

7. You should buy a present _____ your mom. It's her birthday tomorrow.

8. Which restaurant do you want to eat _____? I

9. She has a date _____ May 3rd.

10. Who was the book written _____?

11. Which hotel did he go _____?

12. Which hotel did they stay _____?

13. Do you study _____ a nice teacher?

14. Did you go _____ a beach _____ bus?

15. What are you smiling _____?

Prepositions 13

1. I don't believe _____ ghosts

2. Hold _____ the bar when you ride a roller coaster.

3. Please sign your name _____ the line.

4. What did you talk to him _____?

5. The lights went _____, so we lit _____ a candle.

6. The fire alarm went _____ late _____ night.

7. Put the chicken _____ the oven.

8. Your English is getting better day _____ day.

9. If you want to eat _____ KFC, I will pay _____ you.

10. Don't forget to bring your book _____ you to this class.

11. What did you do _____ your holidays?

12. I spend a lot of time _____ my friends _____ a park _____ my home.

13. I hope you get all of the answers right _____ the test.

14. This chair was made _____ Thailand, and is made _____ wood.

15. Please take your wet socks _____ your feet.

Prepositions 14

1. Please take _____ your hat and sit _____ the table.

2. The plane landed _____ PET Airport _____ Moscow.

3. She woke _____ _____ Sunday morning _____ 8am.

4. He dresses _____ a suit when he goes _____ work.

5. The girl dove _____ the pool early _____ the morning.

6. Rex escaped _____ the fire.

7. How do you feel _____ this car? It is _____ sale.

8. Hana is really good _____ swimming. She swims _____ a fish.

9. I need some help _____ my homework.

10. Edison was the inventor _____ the light bulb.

11. Don't come _____ here. Keep _____!

12. You look tired. Why don't you take _____ your shoes and lie _____.

13. _____ fall, leaves are all _____ my house.

14. You made 5 mistakes _____ your test, so you got a B _____ the test.

15. The test is _____. Please hand _____ your papers right now.

Prepositions 15

Fill in the blank
Write a proper preposition for each sentence. Sometimes, there is more than one answer.

1. Monkeys live _____ trees.

2. People talk _____ the telephone _____ their friends.

3. I talked _____ my mom yesterday, but she was _____ a hurry.

4. I watched a hockey game _____ TV yesterday. My team won _____ 2 goals.

5. A saw a plane fly _____ a building.

6. I live _____ the 2nd floor.

7. Why are you looking _____ me?

8. The music is too loud. Please turn _____ the volume.

9. Don't jump _____ the water. It's cold.

10. We study _____ 4 o'clock _____ 5:20.

11. People walk _____ rivers _____ summer nights.

12. There are many stars _____ space.

13. Our feet are _____ the table (or chairs) and _____ our shoes.

14. Put your jacket _____ your chair and sit _____.

15. Please turn the light _____ when you study, and turn _____ the light after you finish.

Prepositions 16

1. I am bored _____ this book. It's not interesting _____ all.

2. You really look _____ your mom.

3. Get _____ the bus. It is leaving _____ 2 minutes.

4. There is a Chinese restaurant _____ the hotel. I go there once _____ a while.

5. I don't like shopping _____ clothes. .

6. _____ the top _____ the mountain, you can see the city.

7. _____ summer, I go _____ a beach, and lie _____ the sand.

8. Your feet are _____ your shoes, and _____ the table.

9. When I wake _____ _____ Sunday morning, I work.

10. I have a pain _____ my arm.

11. Do you get _____ the elevator, or walk _____ the stairs.

12. _____ the morning, people get _____ their cars, and turn them _____.

13. The President _____ the U.S. lives _____ a white house _____ his wife.

14. A car crashed _____ a tree, but the people _____ the car were OK.

15. The answers _____ these questions are not easy _____ you.

Articles Section

Articles 1

Fill in the blanks (a, an, the or X)
Articles are always used before nouns. Common singular nouns (i.e. a car, a chair, an apple) are the most common nouns to articles. Proper nouns (i.e. The Hudson River) sometimes take the article THE, sometimes not. Non-counting nouns and plural nouns also take articles sometimes, if they are known to the speaker (i.e. The water in my glass is hot)

1. I have _____ rice, _____ book, _____ water and _____ onion in my

    _____ bag.

2. I have _____ eraser in my _____ pencil case.

3. _____ Granby Zoo is _____ large place with many _____ animals.

4. I saw _____ elephant and _____ owl in _____ tree.

5. At _____ Sandy Beach, you can find _____ Hyatt Hotel.

6. _____ computer on my desk is new.

7. _____ Golden Bridge was built in _____ 1960.

8. In _____ Hari Park, you can climb up _____ Yuri Mountain.

9. My grandmother had _____ small home near _____ Lake Reri.

10. Many ants live in _____ Sahara Desert.

Articles 2

Fill in the blanks (a, an, the or X)
Articles are always used before nouns. Common singular nouns (i.e. a car, a chair, an apple) are the most common nouns to take articles. Proper nouns (i.e. The Hudson River) sometimes take the article THE, sometimes not. Non-counting nouns and plural nouns also take articles sometimes, if they are known to the speaker (i.e. The water in my glass is hot)

In _____ morning, I always eat _____ apple and _____ orange. Sometimes, if I am such

_____ hungry guy, I go to _____ restaurant by _____ car. At _____ restaurant, I

eat _____ lot of food, so sometimes people look at me in _____ strange way. One day, when

I was at _____ restaurant, _____ strange thing happened. _____ owner of

_____ restaurant told all of _____ customers that he would have _____ contest to see

who could eat _____ most food in _____ short time. Three people wanted to win

_____ contest, and I was one of _____ guys. _____ First guy was from _____

USA. _____ Second guy was from _____ China. And of course, I was _____ last guy in

_____ contest. We had to eat hot-dogs, and I was lucky, because I loved hot-dogs. _____

rules were easy: _____ winner was _____ person who could eat _____ most hot-dogs

in 3 minutes. _____ Owner said, "Ready, set, go," and we all started to eat like _____ crazy

pigs. After 2 minutes, I was feeling _____ little sick, but I really wanted to win. However, I lost

_____ contest, but I ate _____ lots of hot-dogs.

Articles 3

1. _____ Last year, at _____ Christmas, I bought _____ nice gift for my mom.

2. _____ Next time I go to _____ Netherlands, I will visit _____ Van Gogh River.

3. We study on _____ 3rd floor in this _____ building.

4. _____ Most people like to drink coffee in _____ morning.

5. I like smart students _____ most.

6. _____ University of McGill is _____ best university in _____ Canada.

7. I have _____ pencil and _____ eraser.

8. I lived on _____ Benny street in _____ apartment.

9. When I cook in _____ kitchen in my home, I put on _____ old shirt.

10. At _____ night, I saw _____ cat climb up _____ tree.

Articles 4

_____ Smith family is _____ very special family because every person in _____ family is _____ genius. There are two reasons why _____ family is so smart. _____ First reason is that they all drink _____ special juice. _____ Other reason is _____ family studies all _____ time. One day, _____ father told his family, "Today I will make _____ new machine that will help all _____ people clean their homes." Later that night, in _____ secret, _____ father screamed happily. When he came out of _____ room, he was holding _____ ugly, square box. Everybody in _____ family laughed, but when _____ father put _____ box down, _____ box began to move. It moved fast. Really fast. _____ strange light went all over _____ room, and then _____ light went off. When _____ family looked around _____ room, they were shocked. _____ room was so clean. However, there was _____ problem. _____ father did not take _____ showers, so he was very dirty too. When _____ box cleaned _____ room, it also cleaned _____ Mr. Smith away.

Articles 5

My brother is _____ dumb guy. He is in _____ grade 4, and he always plays _____ computer games on his _____ computer. Today, he wanted to go to _____ Gorilla Park to play _____ tennis with _____ girl. _____ Girl is so _____ tall, and she is really smart, so I don't know why she likes my brother. When he got _____ home, he went to _____ bathroom and took _____ shower because he smelled like _____ dirty cat. When he got out of _____ shower, I played _____ trick on him. I told him that _____ girl wanted him to go to _____ Scary Museum. My brother put on _____ pair of pants, he brushed his _____ hair, and ran out _____ front door like _____ cheetah. I saw him get on _____ bus near _____ Nakajima School, and he had _____ huge smile on his face. I think he will be _____ angry boy when he gets home, but I don't care. I am stronger than him.

Articles 6

1. I got _____ bad mark on _____ test, so my mom hit me in _____ shoulder.

2. I have _____ same bag as you, but I want _____ another bag.

3. _____ Philippines has _____ many islands.

4. _____ eagle can fly faster than _____ pigeon.

5. I watched _____ movie Star Wars _____ day before yesterday.

6. I went to _____ Yuki Beach, and _____ Yumi Building 2 days ago.

7. You are _____ most talented student in _____ Yuni University.

8. _____ Mont Fuji has _____ lake and _____ park on it.

9. _____ Ishikari River has _____ lots of _____ fish in it.

10. _____ First time I met my friend, it was _____ cold day in _____ February.

Articles 7

Fill in the blanks (a, an, the or X)
Articles are always used before nouns. Common singular nouns (i.e. a car, a chair, an apple) are the most common nouns to take articles. Proper nouns (i.e. The Hudson River) sometimes take the article THE, sometimes not. Non-counting nouns and plural nouns also take articles sometimes, if they are known to the speaker (i.e. The water in my glass is hot)

Yesterday was _____ very exciting day. When I woke up in _____ morning, I took

_____ shower, put on _____ clothes, and then _____ phone rang. It was my

_____ best friend. He told me that he had won _____ lottery, and that he was now

_____ rich man. I felt great. Then he asked me to take _____ trip with him around

_____ United States and _____ Canada. I said yes. First, we went to _____ PET Airport,

and took _____ plane to Florida. We went to _____ Marine Land, where we saw _____

largest whale in _____ world do some amazing tricks. It splashed _____ people sitting in

_____ first row, and they got very _____ wet. Next, we drove to _____ city of New

York, where we did many great things. We went to _____ Yankee Stadium, _____ Hyper

Museum, _____ Rosy Garden, and _____ Statue of _____ Liberty. _____ Next

Day, we took _____ boat to _____ Port of Montreal. We drove on _____ Highway 15

to _____ Mont Tremblant, and we skied _____ lot. Then my friend bought _____ ski

hill, and he is still there right now.

Articles 8

1. _____ television was _____ great invention.

2. _____ Ostrich puts its head in _____ ground when it is scared.

3. My friend bought _____ guitar for _____ lot of money.

4. However, he can't play _____ guitar at all.

5. If he practices _____ guitar, he will join _____ band called _____ Fishes.

6. In _____ evening, I teach _____ class to some nice students.

7. I call my mother once _____ week.

8. _____ Man in _____ red coat over there looks like _____ Santa.

9. Today I can't go, but I will go _____ next week.

10. Can I have _____ piece of _____ gum?

Articles 9

Fill in the blanks (a, an, the or X)
Articles are always used before nouns. Common singular nouns (i.e. a car, a chair, an apple) are the most common nouns to take articles. Proper nouns (i.e. The Hudson River) sometimes take the article THE, sometimes not. Non-counting nouns and plural nouns also take articles sometimes, if they are known to the speaker (i.e. The water in my glass is hot)

1. _____ St. Lawrence River has many _____ boats on it.

2. _____ Empire State Building in _____ New York is _____ very tall.

3. I took _____ trip to _____ Lake Biwa _____ last year.

4. I have _____ same pen as you, so we are _____ lucky people.

5. I am _____ only person who has _____ car in this _____ class.

6. _____ octopus and _____ apple are not _____ same at all.

7. My friend took _____ airplane at _____ Chitose Airport.

8. _____ Rocky Mountains is in _____ North America.

9. _____ Atlantic Ocean is bigger than _____ Mersey Pond.

10. Once upon _____ time, _____ dinosaurs lived on _____ moon, I think.

Articles 10

Fill in the blanks (a, an, the or X)
Articles are always used before nouns. Common singular nouns (i.e. a car, a chair, an apple) are the most common nouns to take articles. Proper nouns (i.e. The Hudson River) sometimes take the article THE, sometimes not. Non-counting nouns and plural nouns also take articles sometimes, if they are known to the speaker (i.e. The water in my glass is hot)

1. _____ Eiffel Tower was built in _____ 1800s.

2. _____ Great Wall of China is made of stone.

3. _____ Russia is _____ biggest country in _____ world.

4. _____ Osaka Castle is _____ windy place.

5. _____ London Bridge is _____ old bridge

6. _____ Pyramids in Egypt were built in _____ 1st century.

7. _____ capital of Brazil is not Rio de Janeiro.

8. _____ Pacific Ocean is larger than _____ Atlantic Ocean.

9. I ate _____ apple, _____ orange, _____ rice, and _____ eye yesterday.

10. In _____ city of Tokyo, there is _____ building called _____ Sky Tree.

Articles 11

Fill in the blanks (a, an, the or X)
Articles are always used before nouns. Common singular nouns (i.e. a car, a chair, an apple) are the most common nouns to take articles. Proper nouns (i.e. The Hudson River) sometimes take the article THE, sometimes not. Non-counting nouns and plural nouns also take articles sometimes, if they are known to the speaker (i.e. The water in my glass is hot)

_____ first time I went to _____ Korea, in _____ Asia, I took _____ airplane to _____ Kimpo Airport. At _____ airport, _____ man named Mr. Kim was waiting for me. He took me to _____ hotel near _____ Kangnam Station. It was _____ cold, winter day, and I was tired.

I went into _____ room 333 in _____ basement of _____ hotel. That room was my apartment, but it didn't have _____ window or _____ heater. That day, I was _____ cold man. However, _____ next day, I got _____ heater, so I was fine. That day was fun, because I did _____ lots of fun things. I went to _____ Namsan Tower, _____ 63 Building, _____ Chamsil Stadium, _____ Han River, and _____ Inter-Continental Hotel. I'll never forget that day for _____ rest of my life.

Articles 12

_____ Boy won _____ first prize in _____ very strange competition. It was _____ hot-dog eating contest. _____ fastest eater was _____ winner. Many people from around _____ world try to win _____ contest. _____ Last year, Fat Boy Bones, _____ largest man in _____ British Empire, was _____ winner. Bones was _____ boy's rival. On _____ day of _____ contest, Bones and _____ boy had to eat _____ same number of hotdogs: 50. At _____ first, _____ boy was slow, but after 48 hotdogs, Bones stopped eating. He started to turn blue, and fell down. _____ Boy saw what happened, so he hit Bones hard on _____ back. Bones coughed, and started breathing again. _____ Boy was _____ winner, and he was _____ hero. _____ Prize was _____ million dollars, so now _____ boy's family lives in _____ nice home.

Articles 13

Sam Shutt is _____ man who has _____ very sad life. When he was _____ young, he

got lost, and never found his way home. He was swimming at _____ Sandy Beach on _____

East Sea. _____ Large bird picked Sam up, and flew to _____ Monkey Airport in _____

U.S.A. _____ Bird dropped Sam into _____ bag, and then _____ bag was put onto

_____ airplane that went to _____ Montreal. When _____ bag's owners opened

_____, they found _____ baby boy. _____ Police in Montreal looked and looked for

_____ boy's parents. They looked at _____ Bell Center, _____ Alla Shopping Mall,

_____ McGill University, and even _____ Queen Elizabeth Hotel. _____ Police never

found Sam's parents. That was 20 years ago, and still, Sam is _____ lonely man.

Articles 14

Fill in the blanks (a, an, the or X)
Articles are always used before nouns. Common singular nouns (i.e. a car, a chair, an apple) are the most common nouns to take articles. Proper nouns (i.e. The Hudson River) sometimes take the article THE, sometimes not. Non-counting nouns and plural nouns also take articles sometimes, if they are known to the speaker (i.e. The water in my glass is hot)

I watched _____ movie at _____ movie theatre _____ last Saturday. _____ movie was about _____ baseball team that was _____ worst team in _____ China. _____ coach of the team was _____ very tired man, and he always slept at _____ games. _____ team played at _____ Olympic Stadium, and _____ team's name was _____ Squirrels. _____ best player on _____ team was _____ girl. One day, _____ coach of _____ Squirrels had _____ fight with another _____ coach. _____ two coaches decided to play _____ game with their teams. _____ loser of _____ game had to quit _____ coaching forever. In _____ last inning, _____ girl player had to hit _____ home run to win _____ game. She didn't, and _____ movie ended sadly.

Articles 15

1. I went to school at _____ Harvard University.

2. _____ weather in Sapporo is nice.

3. _____ Philippines has many islands.

4. Almost all of _____ people in this house have _____ black hair.

5. _____ first thing I do in _____ morning is wash _____ dishes in _____ sink.

6. At _____ first, I didn't like to eat _____ vegetables, but now I do.

7. What time will _____ next show begin?

8. _____ people in _____ Australia don't like _____ rabbits.

9. I heard that _____ police in Japan don't carry _____ guns.

10. I wonder who invented _____ guitar?

Articles 16

In _____ morning, I always drink _____ glass of water. _____ Doctors say that

_____ water is very good for us. So, I drink _____ lots of water. At _____ night, before

I go to _____ bed, I wash _____ dishes in _____ kitchen, and drink one more

_____ glass of water.

These days, _____ water is making _____ lot of problems in _____ world. Sometimes

_____ flood happens in _____ city, and that damages _____ buildings in _____

city. Or _____ hurricane will drop much water onto _____ city, or even _____ tsunami

can crash into _____ country and hurt many people. Maybe I should buy _____ boat and

take _____ trip around _____ world. I could visit _____ Ireland in _____

Europe. I could sail down _____ Amazon River in _____ Amazon Forest in _____

South America. I could even eat _____ apple and _____ orange near _____ Banana

Mountain.

Lie Game

The sentences below are examples. Students can follow or use them to help make sentences.

Lie Game 1: nouns

APPLE, BEAR, COFFEE

- Apples are bigger than grapes.
- Bears live in deserts.
- Many people drink coffee in the morning.
-
-
-

DENTIST, FIREMAN, GOLFER

- Dentists help people with their teeth.
- Firemen help people cook food.
- Golfers play golf with balls and clubs.
-
-
-

HOSPITAL, JAM, KIWI

- There are about 1, 300 hospitals in Canada.
- Some people eat onion jam.
- Kiwis don't grow in Italy.
-
-
-

FURNITURE, LETTUCE, MEAT

- A lot of furniture is made of gold.
- Lettuce tastes delicious in summer.
- People in Australia can eat kangaroo meat.
-
-
-

Lie Game 2: verbs

ASK, BAKE, CALL

- Students ask questions to teachers.
- Bakers bake bread.
- The sun is called *La Lune* in French.
-
-
-

FIX, GRAB, HELP

- Doctors are good at fixing televisions.
- It is not good to grab food on a table.
- Policemen help people who are in trouble.
-
-
-

JOKE, KICK, LAUGH

- On TV, we can watch people telling jokes.
- Soccer players can kick balls hard.
- It is good to laugh when people fall down.
-
-
-

NEED, OPEN, PUSH

- Plants need water to live.
- If it is hot in a room, open a window.
- Pushing people in Africa is a nice thing to do.
-
-
-

Lie Game 3: adjectives

ANGRY, BORING, CALM

- Teachers get angry when students study hard.
- This book is not boring.
- Calm people are sometimes quiet.
-
-
-

DUMB, EASY, FUNNY

- It isn't nice to call people "dumb".
- Making perfect sentences in English is easy.
- Funny movies sometimes make people cry.
-
-
-

GREAT, HAPPY, INTERESTING

- England is a part of Great Britain.
- People feel happy when they are sick.
- People like to read interesting books.
-
-
-

JEALOUS, KIND, LOUD

- Some people are jealous of rich people.
- Sometimes, it's not easy to be kind to your brothers or sisters.
- Loud music doesn't hurt your ears.
-
-
-

Lie Game 4: adverbs

QUIETLY, SLOWLY, WELL

- Elephants walk quietly.
- Turtles don't swim slowly.
- Monkeys climb trees well.

-
-
-

FAST, NICELY, BEAUTIFULLY

- Hungry people eat fast.
- Monsters talk nicely.
- Ballet dancers move beautifully.

-
-
-

ALWAYS, USUALLY, NEVER

- It always rains in Tokyo in June.
- Usually, European countries win the World Cup.
- Snakes never eat chickens.

-
-
-

WHEN, AS SOON AS, THE NEXT TIME

- Babies cry when they are happy.
- As soon as it rains, people usually use their umbrellas.
- The next time you are thirsty, you should drink some water.

-
-
-

Lie Game 5: pronouns

ME, MY, MINE

- "People tell me I am short," said a giant.
- "My feet are very small. You can't see them," said a snake
- "My favorite hero is Spiderman," said a spider.
-
-
-

WE, I, MYSELF

- "We need to help other people," said a very bad man.
- "I like to swim," said a fish.
- "I sometimes talk to myself," said a man who lived alone in a cave.
-
-
-

ANYTHING, THIS, ANOTHER

- "I don't have anything in my pocket," said a man with no pants.
- "This is very hot," said a lady holding ice.
- "I have 3 friends. One is tall, another is small, and the other is bald," said a funny man.
-
-
-

EVERYTHING, EVERY OTHER, THE PERSON WHO

- Nobody knows everything.
- Some students go to school on Saturday every other week.
- The person who helps sick people is called a teacher.
-
-
-

Lie Game 6: prepositions

IN, ON, UNDER

- Fish live in the oceans.
- People live on the moon.
- Worms live under the ground.

-

-

-

BETWEEN, NEXT TO, IN FRONT OF

- The letter x is between w and y.
- The air is fresh next to a garbage can.
- If a park is in front of your home, maybe it is loud on sunny days.

-

-

-

BEHIND, ABOVE, OVER

- Slow runners run behind fast runners.
- Airplanes never fly above clouds.
- Bridges go over rivers.

-

-

-

WITH, FOR, BY

- When people travel to another country, they bring money with them.
- It is difficult for babies to climb trees.
- Elephants like to live by themselves, not in groups with other elephants.

-

-

-

Lie Game 7: irregular verbs

BEGIN, CATCH, DO

- In Brazil, winter begins in June.
- People like to catch colds.
- Sometimes, students do homework in the morning.
-
-
-

EAT, FORGET, GIVE

- Frogs eat bugs.
- Old people never forget things.
- Policemen give tickets to fast drivers.
-
-
-

HAVE, LEND, MAKE

- Some birds have 4 eyes.
- Banks lend money to people.
- It is not easy to make good friends.
-
-
-

RUN, SEND, TAKE

- Some kangaroos can run faster than horses.
- Some companies send rockets into space.
- Clean people take a bath or shower once a week.
-
-
-

Lie Game 8: comparatives & superlatives

BIGGER THAN, CLEANER THAN, MORE FUN

- France is bigger than Russia.
- In general, pigs are cleaner than dogs.
- Games are usually more fun than homework.
- ....
- ....
- ....

BETTER THAN, SAFER THAN, HARDER THAN

- Most people think chocolate ice cream tastes better than banana ice cream.
- A volcano is safer than a swimming pool.
- Gold is harder than plastic.
- ....
- ....
- ....

THE TALLEST, THE MOST INTELLIGENT, THE STRONGEST

- The tallest mountain in the world is in Nepal.
- The most intelligent dogs are chihuahuas.
- The dung beetle is the strongest insect in the world
- ....
- ....
- ....

THE MOST EXPENSIVE, THE LARGEST, THE HARDEST

- The most expensive cars in the world are sports cars.
- The largest planet is Mars.
- A diamond is the hardest stone.
- ....
- ....
- . ...

Making Perfect Questions

MPQ 1

For each sentence, write a question that answers it. For example, if the sentence is "I brush my teeth 3 times a day", the question could be "How often do you brush your teeth?" Many questions can be used for each sentence.

1.   It is cold today.

_____

2.   I am angry because you stepped on my foot.

_____

3.   I usually drink a glass of water in the morning.

_____

4.   I came to Sapporo by airplane.

_____

5.   I eat rice every day.

_____

6.   Today is Thursday, so I am happy.

_____

7.   On March 14.

_____

8.   The expensive car is mine.

_____

9.   I like apples more than bananas.

_____

10. He talks very quickly.

_____

MPQ 2

For each sentence, write a question that answers it.

1. The cat is white.

_____

2. It is on the wall.

_____

3. I'll go home in a few minutes.

_____

4. He is studying right now.

_____

5. I weigh 83kg.

_____

6. If I am busy, I don't eat supper.

_____

7. This pen costs 4 dollars.

_____

8. I don't like this chair because it is uncomfortable.

_____

9. No, I don't.

_____

10. Yes, I am.

_____

MPQ 3

For each sentence, write a question that answers it.

1. I always wake up early in the morning.

_____

2. I don't know who called me yesterday.

_____

3. No, I can't speak French very well.

_____

4. My dentist is a nice man.

_____

5. I only have 1 dollar in my pocket.

_____

6. Yes, she will.

_____

7. No, I haven't.

_____

8. The water is too cold, so I don't want to go swimming.

_____

9. We will study 1 hour longer.

_____

10. This movie is 2 hours long.

_____

MPQ 4

For each sentence, write a question that answers it.

1. We start studying at 5 o'clock in the evening.

_____

2. I have one sister.

_____

3. It took me 5 minutes to come here today.

_____

4. I think I am a good singer.

_____

5. Today is my birthday.

_____

6. Yes, you should.

_____

7. I want to go to Vancouver next winter.

_____

8. I live very close to here.

_____

9. There is a hospital next to my house.

_____

10. We study on the 2nd floor.

_____

MPQ 5

For each sentence, write a question that answers it.

1. No, she couldn't.

_____

2. Tomorrow is my birthday.

_____

3. It is 10:05.

_____

4. I'm going to wear my pink pants to the party.

_____

5. I think he is sleeping.

_____

6. That guy is the fastest runner in this class.

_____

7. That's my yellow book.

_____

8. I woke up at 7am this morning.

_____

9. I don't like winter because it is too cold.

_____

10. I live on the 2nd floor.

_____

MPQ 6

For each sentence, write a question that answers it.

1. No, he didn't.

_____

2. I came here on foot.

_____

3. This class is 1 hour and a half long.

_____

4. I would like to play with the yellow ball.

_____

5. No, I haven't.

_____

6. I like my steak medium-well.

_____

7. If it rains, I will stay home tomorrow.

_____

8. It cost $5.

_____

9. That is called *bicycle* in English.

_____

10. I lived there for 6 years.

_____

MPQ 7

For each sentence, write a question that answers it.

1. Grrrphlattherbrotdddd!

   _____

2. He said that he liked bananas.

   _____

3. My dog weighs 8kg.

   _____

4. Ichiro is a baseball player.

   _____

5. He was born in Japan.

   _____

6. He played for the Mariners.

   _____

7. He is about 170 cm tall.

   _____

8. I think he is a nice man.

   _____

9. I always drink coffee when I wake up in the morning.

   _____

10. My favourite colour is green.

   _____

MPQ 8

For each sentence, write a question that answers it.

1. Yes, it does.

_____

2. I use the Internet 2 times a week.

_____

3. She is in the hospital.

_____

4. Her doctor's name is Dr. Frankenshine.

_____

5. He studied at Waseda University.

_____

6. He has 2 children.

_____

7. He drives a fancy car.

_____

8. She will leave the hospital in 3 days.

_____

9. Her knee hurts a lot, so she will have surgery.

_____

10. My dog likes pizza.

_____

Making Perfect Sentences

MPS 1

Write a sentence using each word.

I	
you	
he	
she	
we	
they	
it	
this	
that	
these	

MPS 2

	Write a sentence using each word.

pencil	
cry	
go	
sometimes	
shave	
carry	
shower	
talk	
fruit	
vegetables	

MPS 3

Write a sentence using each word.

on Friday	
in the morning	
at night	
from	
warm	
slowly	
quietly	
chilly	
foggy	
rain	

MPS 4

Write a sentence using each word.

before	
up	
because	
so	
but	
can	
like…ing	
like to	
smile	
clap	

MPS 5

Write a sentence using each word.

everyday	
right now	
last	
long	
two days ago	
tonight	
next week	
pair of	
rabbit	
Chinese	

MPS 6

	Write a sentence using each word.

can	
will	
had to	
must	
above	
near	
outside	
inside	
between	
meat	

MPS 7

gold	
rice	
whale	
ask	
people	
borrow	
a fish	
a calendar	
dragon	
dream	

MPS 8

Write a sentence using each word.

money	
mail	
traffic	
some	
a few	
plenty of	
hotel	
computer	
a piece of	
one of	

MPS 9

those	
home	
mother	
father	
homework	
food	
run	
inside	
noodles	
never	

MPS 10

	Write a sentence using each word.

hard	
as fast as	
quickly	
windy	
elephant	
sneeze	
coughed	
softly	
smelly	
need	

MPS 11

Write a sentence using each word.

would	
could	
should	
may	
might	
meet	
spoon	
knife	
fork	
chopsticks	

MPS 12

Write a sentence using each word.

them	
cut	
feet	
teeth	
furniture	
round	
rough	
some	
any	
every	

MPS 13

Write a sentence using each word.

tomorrow	
these days	
last month	
people	
my family	
small	
the smallest	
today	
yesterday	
next week	

MPS 14

Write a sentence using each word.

2 years	
before	
salty	
special	
listen	
touch	
on	
next to	
after	
well	

MPS 15

Write a sentence using each word.

talented	
honest	
spaghetti	
in	
under	
beautiful	
intelligent	
interesting	
tall	
yellow	

MPS 16

Write a sentence using each word.

plastic	
funny	
good	
expensive	
handsome	
quiet	
new	
candy	
boring	
neat	

MPS 17

Write a sentence using each word.

badly	
3 hours ago	
the day after tomorrow	
nice	
pork	
in front of	
over	
below	
in 2 days	
the day before yesterday	

MPS 18

Write a sentence using each word.

lately	
water	
sugar	
across	
above	
along	
between	
off	
usually	
sometimes	

133

MPS 19

Write a sentence using each word.

seldom	
nowadays	
in a while	
below	
up	
always	
often	
rarely	
almost never	
soon	

MPS 20

Write a sentence using each word.	
every other day	
the news	
the Philippines	
Japanese	
was studying	
french fries	
her	
she	
tell	
will go	

Writing: Short Stories

Short Story 1

THE LUCKY COIN

PICTURE

Short Story 2

THE TIME MACHINE

PICTURE

Short Story 3

DOCTOR STRANGE

PICTURE

Short Story 4

THE TADA TREE

PICTURE

Short Story 5

MOON CAMP

PICTURE

Short Story 6

MUSIC GIRL

PICTURE

Short Story 7

MR. FISH

PICTURE

Short Story 8

THE LONELY MONKEY

PICTURE

Appendix

LIST OF PREPOSITIONS

Prepositions are words that tells us about where something is, or when something happens. They are always used to talk about nouns, like **on** TV, **in** my hand, or **above** my head. Here is a list of common prepositions:

aboard	about	above	across	After	against
ahead of	all over	along	among	Apart	around
as	at	away	away from	Back	before
behind	below	beneath	between	beyond	by
close by	close to	despite	down	during	except
for	forward	from	in	in between	in front
inside	into	like	near	next to	of
off	on	on top of	opposite	outside	onto
over	out	out of	round	Past	since
through	to	toward	towards	under	until
upon	up	with	within	without	

OSASCNM – THE ORDER OF ADJECTIVES

In English, you must use adjectives in the certain order in a sentence. You must not mix up the order of the adjectives. It is one of English grammar rules.

If you can remember OSASCNM, then you will know the order of adjectives.

<u>O</u> = Opinion, <u>S</u> = Size, <u>A</u> = Age, <u>S</u> = Shape, <u>C</u> = Colour, <u>N</u> = Nationality, <u>M</u> = Material

◎ I have a <u>nice</u>, <u>big</u>, <u>old</u>, <u>square</u>, <u>brown</u>, <u>Canadian</u>, <u>wooden</u> chair.
      O   S   A   S   C   N   M

× I have a <u>big</u>, <u>square</u>, <u>Canadian</u>, <u>old</u>, <u>brown</u>, <u>nice</u> <u>wooden</u> chair.
      S   S   N   A   C   O   M

Present	Past	P. Perfect	Present	Past	P. Perfect	Present	Past	P. Perfect
awake	awoke	awoken	come	came	come	freeze	froze	frozen
Be	was/were	been	cost	cost	cost	get	got	gotten
			creep	crept	crept	give	gave	given
bear	bore	born	cut	cut	cut	go	went	gone
beat	beat	beat	deal	dealt	dealt	grind	ground	ground
become	became	become	dig	dug	dug	grow	grew	grown
begin	began	begun	dive	dived/dove	dived	hang	hung	hung
bend	bent	bent				hear	heard	heard
beset	beset	beset	do	did	done	hide	hid	hidden
bet	bet	bet	draw	drew	drawn	hit	hit	hit
bid	bid/bade	bid/bidden	dream	dreamt/dreamed/	dreamt/dreamed	hold	held	held
						hurt	hurt	hurt
bind	bound	bound	drive	drove	driven	keep	kept	kept
bite	bit	bitten	drink	drank	drunk	kneel	knelt	knelt
bleed	bled	bled	eat	ate	eaten	knit	knit	knit
blow	blew	blown	fall	fell	fallen	know	knew	know
break	broke	broken	feed	fed	fed	lay	laid	laid
breed	bred	bred	feel	felt	felt	lead	led	led
bring	brought	brought	fight	fought	fought	leap leaped/	leapt leaped/	leapt
broadcast	broadcast	broadcast	find	found	found			
build	built	built	fit	fit	fit	learn learned/	learnt/learned	/learnt
burn	Burned/burnt	burned/burnt	flee	fled	fled			
			fling	flung	flung	leave	left	left
burst	burst	burst	fly	flew	flown	lend	lent	lent
buy	bought	bought	forbid	forbade	forbidden	lie	lay	lain
cast	cast	cast	forget	forgot	forgotten	light	lighted/lit	lighted
catch	caught	caught	forego	forewent	foregone			
choose	chose	chosen	forgive	forgave	forgiven	lose	lost	lost

cling	clung	clung	forsake	forsook	forsaken	make	made	made
mean	meant	meant	sew	sewed/sewn	sewed/sewn	spend	spent	spent
meet	met	met				spin	spun	spun
misspell	misspelled/ misspelt	misspelled/ misspelt	shake	shook	shaken	spit spit	/spat	spit
			shave shaved	shaved/	shaven			
mistake	mistook	mistaken				split	split	split
mow	mowed	mowed/ mown	shear	shore	shorn	spread	spread	spread
			shed	shed	shed	Spring sprang/	sprung	sprung
overcome	overcame	overcome	shine	shone	shone			
overdo	overdid	overdone	shoe shoed	shoed/	shod	stand	stood	stood
overtake	overtook	overtaken				steal	stole	stolen
overthrow	overthrew	overthrown	shoot	shot	shot	stick	stuck	stuck
pay	paid	paid	show showed	showed/	shown	sting	stung	stung
plead	pled	pled				stink	stank	stunk
prove	proved	proved/ proven	shrink	shrank	shrunk	stride	strode	stridden
			shut	shut	shut	string	strung	strung
put	put	put	sing	sang	sung	strive	strove	striven
read	read	read	sink	sank	sunk	swear	swore	sworn
rid	rid	rid	sit	sat	sat	sweep	swept	swept
ride	rode	ridden	sleep	slept	slept	swell swelled	swelled/	swollen
ring	rang	rung	slay	slew	slain			
rise	rose	risen	slide	slid	slid	swim	swam	swum
run	ran	run	sling	slung	slung	swing	swung	swung
saw	sawed	sawed/ sawn	slit	slit	slit	take	took	taken
			smite	smote	smitten	teach	taught	taught
say	said	said	sow sowed	sowed/	sown	tear	tore	torn
see	saw	seen				tell	told	told
seek	sought	sought	speak	spoke	spoken	think	thought	thought
sell	sold	sold	speed	sped	sped	thrive thrived/	throve	thrived
send	sent	sent	spill	spilt	spilt			

set	set	set	spilled/	spilled/		throw	threw	thrown
thrust	thrust	thrust	wed	wed	wed	withhold	withheld	withheld
tread	trod	trodden	weave weaved/	wove / weaved	woven	withstand	withstood	withstood
understand	understood	understood				wring	wrung	wrung
upset	upset	upset	weep	wept	wept	write	wrote	written
wake	woke	woken	wind	wound	wound			
wear	wore	worn	win	won	won			

www.ingramcontent.com/pod-product-compliance
Lightning Source LLC
Chambersburg PA
CBHW081425090426
42740CB00017B/3188